Old Dunkeld and Birnam

P. J. G. Ransom

Dunkeld Cathedral in 1878.

Acknowledgments

I have received much help from the following, to whom I am most grateful: Ian Abbott, Dunkeld and Birnam Historical Society; Jane Anderson, Archivist, Blair Castle; Yvonne Bell and other staff of Local Studies Department, A.K. Bell Library, Perth; Joan Brookes, Dunkeld Community Archive; Anne Cadden, The New School; Bob Flockhart, authority on vintage vehicles; Baroness Linklater; Anne Steuart Fothringham; Thomas Steuart Fothringham.
I am also grateful for the support of my agent, Duncan McAra, and particularly for the support of my wife Elisabeth, who has done so much of the research.

Further Reading

The books listed below were used by the author during his research. Most are unavailable from Stenlake Publishing; please contact your local bookshop or reference library.
Dunkeld and Birnam: Gateway to the Highlands, Dunkeld & Birnam Mercantile Association, 1923
Leslie's Directory for Perth and Perthshire, D. Leslie, 1899 and 1923
Cox, E., (ed.), *Dunkeld Remembered*, Dunkeld and Birnam Historical Society, 1993
Gifford, J., *Perth & Kinross in 'The Buildings of Scotland' series*, Yale University Press, 2007
Haynes, N., *Perth & Kinross: An Illustrated Architectural Guide*, Rutland Press, 2000
Jackson, H., *Niel Gow's Inver*, Perth & Kinross Libraries, 2000
Lane, M., *The Tale of Beatrix Potter*, Frederick Warne & Co. Ltd, 1946
Paxton, R., & Shipway, J., *Civil Engineering Heritage: Scotland Lowlands and Borders*, Thomas Telford Ltd, 2007
Rosenfeld, J., & Smith, A., *Millais*, Tate Publishing, 2007
Ross, D., *The Highland Railway*, Stenlake Publishing Ltd, 2010
Sutherland, D., *Rohallion*, William Heinemann Ltd, 1978
Tranter, N., *The Heartland*, Hodder & Stoughton, 1971

The substantial war memorial for Dunkeld and Birnam was placed on top of a knoll overlooking Little Dunkeld Kirk and the River Tay. This open view would not last: in 1930 the new building for the Royal School of Dunkeld was built on the land in front of the kirk. The knoll itself has become largely covered in woodland which conceals the memorial from below, although it remains in view from Dunkeld Bridge. This picture gives little indication of the memorial's elevated position, nor of its size – it stands some 27 feet high. Hidden from view too is the plaque listing the names of the 74 men from the district who lost their lives during the First World War. Since the time of this photograph, two more plaques have been added which list the 24 men killed during the Second World War and one who was killed in Northern Ireland in 1973.

Introduction

Dunkeld lies at the entrance to the Highlands. Here for the first time the northbound traveller finds that handsome hills are no longer just the view ahead, but are all around. Here too the broad River Tay emerges from between the hills, its valley forming the route to the North. Here yet again the northbound traveller used to cross the cultural divide of the Highland Line – it was just north of Dunkeld that, formerly, he or she first encountered the Gaelic language.

Dunkeld has been of religious significance since the days of St Columba. The monastery established by his followers was eventually replaced by the cathedral built in the fourteenth and fifteenth centuries. But its presence was no guarantee of peace: on the contrary, Dunkeld's location made it of strategic importance from the earliest times. The most recent example of horrific violence came in 1689. Jacobites attacked government troops loyal to William and Mary who were garrisoned in the town, and during the ensuing Battle of Dunkeld the entire town, except for three houses and the cathedral, was burned to ashes. Many of the houses set on fire by one side or the other – accounts differ – had their occupants locked inside to be burned with them. This was a bloodthirsty period in Scottish history: the Battle of Killiecrankie occurred just a few weeks before the one at Dunkeld and within three years there was the massacre at Glencoe. The part of Dunkeld which lay west of the Cathedral was not rebuilt.

The superiority of Dunkeld was held by the bishops until 1704 when the Dukes of Atholl took over. It seems that the former bishop's palace was altered and improved to become a handsome residence, with successive dukes dividing their time between it and Blair Castle – but it was not handsome enough for the fourth duke who, in 1828, started work on a new and much grander house, and pulled down the existing one. Unfortunately when he died in 1830 it was found that there were insufficient funds to complete the new house; eventually its shell too was demolished. In the meantime an inn, surviving from the old town, had been improved and named St Adamnan's Cottage (St Adamnan being one of the early saints associated with the district) for temporary use by the ducal family. But it became their residence at Dunkeld for the remainder of the century. It can be seen, lower right in the adjoining picture.

Successive dukes were concerned to enhance the natural beauties of their surroundings by, for instance, building follies and planting trees – the latter on a large scale. And they were happy to share the beauties of their pleasure grounds with others. Late eighteenth-century tourists such as Thomas Pennant and Sarah Murray came, saw and enthused, to be followed in due course by many, many more.

They were encouraged by gradual improvements in communications. Originally roads in the modern sense were unknown: Dunkeld Cathedral, despite its immense size, had to be built of stones small enough to be carried to the site by packhorses. The first substantial improvements came with construction of military roads in the eighteenth century. But the broad and sometimes turbulent Tay was still crossed by ferries – there were three at Dunkeld within a mile of each other – until 1809 when Dunkeld Bridge was completed. It was one of the earliest works of the Parliamentary Commissioners for Highland Roads and Bridges and was designed by their engineer, Thomas Telford, although in this instance the driving force seems to have been the fourth Duke of Atholl. Although the government contributed £5,000 towards the cost, all or most of the total balance of more than £30,000 was paid by the duke, against the right to charge tolls from users – which would eventually lead to trouble. The duke also acted as contractor for the bridge. In addition to this, he also built the new main road leading northwards from the bridge: this crossed the existing main street at right-angles and, lined in due course with new buildings and hotels, led to a conspicuous change in Dunkeld's layout and appearance.

Dunkeld and bridge from the cathedral.

The sixth duke was much less helpful when it came to further improvements. He objected to railways in the Highlands, and when the Perth & Dunkeld Railway was opened in 1856 its terminus was of necessity outside Atholl lands and three-quarters of a mile short of Dunkeld itself. He took a lot of persuasion before the line could be extended to Inverness in 1863, becoming the main line of the Highland Railway..

Observant readers will have noted that so far there has been no reference to Birnam. That is because before the 1840s Birnam consisted of little more than the well-known reference in Shakespeare's *Macbeth*. Its establishment as a village was the work of Sir William Stewart (later generations would adopt the name Steuart Fothringham), who was proprietor of Murthly Castle, and whose estate marched with that of Atholl to the north. He attempted to found a new village at the northern extremity of his estate in the 1840s but there were no takers. It was only after the railway, of which he was naturally a great supporter, had been opened that he was able successfully to establish the village of Birnam. Like Dunkeld, this also lay on the main road from Perth to the North.

Sir William's intention was particularly to attract wealthy visitors who could now reach Birnam easily and a great many – wealthy and otherwise – took the opportunity to do so. Some stayed in his palatial new hotel, but it also became the practice for the wealthy of late Victorian times to rent entire villas or country houses for the autumn, during the shooting and fishing season. In this manner Rupert Potter and, more particularly, his daughter Beatrix became familiar with the locality, and Sir John Everett Millais, then considered the greatest of British artists, rented a house every autumn for eighteen years during the 1870s and 1880s. The outcome was his famous series of landscapes painted in the district.

That is the stage of development reached by Dunkeld, Birnam and the surrounding area at the period when the photographs reproduced here were taken, with the addition of motor vehicles starting to appear on empty roads. There have been subsequent changes of course – where once there were houses, for instance, now there are parked cars, and where once there were gardens, now there are houses. A greater change has been one specific to a location on an important transport artery. Those empty roads soon filled up and by the 1960s the entire traffic of the A9 was grinding its way through Birnam and Dunkeld. Relief eventually came in 1977 when they were bypassed by the improved A9. The village of Inver nearby, however, which had once with its ferry been a nodal point of the military road network, but had been left a quiet backwater after construction of Dunkeld Bridge, now found that the new A9 sliced right through it. It is to be hoped that further improvements to the A9, currently being planned, will be made with due consideration for the localities through which it passes, as well as for the needs of long-distance traffic.

The oldest part of Murthly Castle is the tower in the background of this photograph. It dates from the sixteenth century, and has been added to (and, on occasion, had additions removed from it) many times over the centuries. The central feature here is the entrance block added in the 1730s, with curved stairways leading up to the entrance itself. This continues to be the front door today, but the stone-built 'lean-to' on the left, which contained a servery corridor, has been demolished.

Dunkeld Cathedral, on the site of earlier monastic buildings, was built in stages between the early fourteenth and early sixteenth centuries. Then in 1560 over-ardent reformers trashed the interior and removed the roof: fortunately they stopped short of setting fire to the building. The choir (extreme right of picture) was restored and re-roofed about 1600 to become the parish church. Further restoration of the choir followed at intervals, often through the intercession of successive Dukes of Atholl. Meanwhile, the bell tower was re-roofed in 1762 and the clock installed in 1814. The nave remained open to the sky, repaired from time to time to prevent collapse of the walls, and used as a burial ground. That was the stage reached by the date of this photograph from the 1870s and it remains in essence the position today.

According to the minister of Dunkeld writing in the *Statistical Account* of the 1790s, Alexander Stewart Earl of Buchan and Badenoch, became known as the 'Wolf of Badenoch' due to his 'ferocious and sanguinary disposition'. His career included being excommunicated, but evidently by his death in 1394 he had demonstrated repentance enough to merit burial within the choir of Dunkeld Cathedral. His sarcophagus, surmounted by his recumbent armoured figure, carved in stone, is seen here. Alongside, on the floor, is the damaged effigy of Bishop William Sinclair, under whose direction the choir was built in the fourteenth century. Neither is in its original position and both, since this photograph was taken, have been moved to other positions nearby at the east end of the choir. Mounted on the east wall of the choir, to the left of the effigy and sarcophagus, is the large marble monument to soldiers of the Black Watch which was unveiled in 1872.

'A nice, snug little cottage' was how Queen Victoria described the Duchess of Atholl's cottage at Dunkeld when she came to stay in 1865, and she delighted her hostess when she enjoyed the haggis which was served. The two women were old friends and, both recently widowed, seem to have enjoyed each other's company so much that the queen returned a year later. One of the highlights of that visit seems to have been a dance for servants and gillies – 'the fiddlers played in very good time, and the dancing was very animated… nothing but reels,' noted the queen. The servants are seen here lined up in front of the cottage, which lay between the cathedral and the River Tay. It was used by members of the duke's family after demolition of old Dunkeld House in 1828/29, and particularly by Duchess Anne who made it her home as dowager after the death of the sixth duke in 1864. When the new Dunkeld House was built in 1898–1900 the cottage was in turn demolished.

Looking east along Cathedral Street. This links the cathedral, behind the photographer, with The Cross and the High Street which can be seen in the distance. It is this part of the town which was rebuilt during the years following the battle, and fire, of 1689. By 1953 many of the houses were in bad condition and extensive demolition was proposed. This fate was averted in 1954 when the National Trust for Scotland accepted two groups of houses, in Cathedral Street and The Cross, to ensure their future preservation, as it considered them to be among the most outstanding architectural compositions in Scotland. Eventually the houses on the north side of Cathedral Street (on the left in this picture) were restored by the National Trust and those on the south by Perth & Kinross County Council, and the restorations received an award from the Saltire Society. Recent architectural guides have been a little hesitant about authenticity, but nevertheless the whole project seems an astonishing achievement considering that it took place at a period when building a brave new world was generally taking precedence over restoring an old and shabby one.

The open space called The Cross narrows to become the High Street. The fountain, still prominent today, was erected by public subscription in 1866 as a memorial to the sixth Duke of Atholl and replaced a market cross. It incorporated drinking fountains for people and for animals. Around it children played on summer evenings and sometimes there were more formal entertainments such as funfairs and circuses.

High Street, looking west towards The Cross. The photograph can be dated to the late 1940s by the two delivery vans – an Austin on the left, a Ford on the right – not to mention the ladies' fashions. The Ford van has a pull-out rear roof and so may have been used as a travelling shop. The Perth Arms was even then old-established, for it had been in business since the 1890s at least and its buildings are possibly a century older still. The ornate building in the right background, built in 1853/54, was originally the Duchess of Atholl's Girls Industrial School, established by Duchess Anne. Later it became the armoury for the Scottish Horse (the yeomanry regiment associated with the district), and later still the kirk hall.

Long ago, when Dunkeld was aligned west - east before Dunkeld Bridge was built, travellers to the east left the town via this brae. Later it became known as Brae Street and it can be glimpsed in the distance on page 9. When snow fell in winter it was a popular place for children to go tobogganing. Cars now park on the sites of the houses on the left.

So well-proportioned is Telford's bridge over the Tay – seen here across the roofs of Dunkeld – that photographs seldom convey its size: at the centre span the road is about 54 feet above usual water level. The whole bridge is some 685 feet long, Telford's largest in Scotland, and was built between 1804 and 1809. The river hereabouts is normally shallow with many shoals, and according to Paxton and Shipway this enabled the bridge to be built successively in two halves in the dry, with the water flow being diverted away from each half while it was being built. The deserted appearance of the bridge seen here did not survive into the motor age, with the road carrying all the heavy traffic of the A9 between the South and Inverness. Relief came in 1977 when Dunkeld was bypassed by new A9 trunk road.

Travellers heading north over Dunkeld Bridge first encountered on their right the Atholl Arms Hotel. This was built in 1833 and became a popular halting place for Victorian tourists, particularly those under the guidance of Thomas Cook's agent. This view dates from 1900; a few years later Baedeker noted that a room could be had for 2s 6d, and dinner from 3s. To its right the hotel is flanked by the Dunkeld Free Church of 1875 (now Dunkeld Antiques) and further to the right again is Watt's Temperance Hotel, now and for many years past the Taybank Hotel (licensed!).

To obtain this view in 1933, the photographer had positioned himself in the middle of the main road coming down off Dunkeld Bridge, looking north up Bridge Street with Atholl Street beyond – the new road built by the Duke of Atholl after construction of the bridge. Bridge House on the left had been a dwelling since it was built soon after the bridge itself, until 1925 when Walker's Pharmacy moved in, having had to leave premises elsewhere in Dunkeld where it had been established for some forty years. By the early 1920s the Atholl Arms had been acquired by Trust Houses Ltd, like many other country town hotels. Trust Houses installed electric light and central heating, and by the time of this picture a small conservatory had appeared, although it has since disappeared. The hotel remains popular today. On the right at the end of the bridge parapet is a telephone kiosk of the K1 type, introduced in the 1920s and preceding the later, familiar, red telephone kiosk. The K1 kiosk was built from pre-cast concrete and had a wooden-framed door.

The Royal Hotel stood and stands on the north side of Atholl Street, although its garage entrance seen here has been filled in. In this view from around 1945 a Hillman Minx is emerging from the garage and an Austin Seven Ruby saloon is parked further down the street. In earlier times this had been a coaching inn and as recently as the early twentieth century, throughout the summer a coach left daily for Braemar complete with scarlet-coated and top-hatted coachman and guard. It travelled via Blairgowrie and Spittal of Glenshee, a full day's journey but evidently still competitive with the roundabout route by train.

A new bridge and a new road evidently demanded a new entrance for Dunkeld House and the fourth Duke of Atholl had this one built in 1809. The gateway itself is flanked by two gate lodges all in the same ornate castellated, mock-defensive gothic style which was popular at the time. By the date of this photograph, 1905, the gateway had already outlived both the house it was built to guard and its intended replacement, which had been left incomplete after the duke's death. Instead it formed the approach to a third house illustrated in the next picture. The entrance buildings remain largely unchanged today, but the kilted and bearded retainer has given way to a discrete notice announcing that you are approaching a Hilton hotel.

A new Dunkeld House was built for the seventh Duke of Atholl in 1898–1900: the site chosen overlooked the River Tay a mile west of Dunkeld itself and was approached by a drive across parkland from the existing gateway. The house is seen here when still quite new, yet it did not remain in Atholl ownership for very long. By the mid 1930s it was unoccupied, and in 1936 it and its policies were sold by Atholl Estates to Sir A.M.P. Lyle, Bart. Around 1970 the house was converted into a luxury hotel and extended in due course, and as such – after a few changes of ownership – it remains.

This is the southern approach to Inver, in the days when horses and carts were more common than the caravans for which the location is now popular. On the left is part of an extensive and old-established sawmill, driven by water power from the nearby River Braan. There were also a meal mill, a lint mill and a waulk mill, the latter for washing wool after it had been spun. In the background is The Square, the buildings of which incorporated an inn. Probably it was there that, a century or so before this picture was taken, the first stagecoach between Inverness and Perth would halt for a while for the celebrated fiddle player Niel Gow, by then elderly, to entertain the passengers.

Niel Gow moved into this cottage at Inver about 1750 and it remained his home until his death 57 years later. Here he worked as a hand-loom weaver, kept cows and played the fiddle. As a young man he had shown sufficient talent to perform before Bonnie Prince Charlie and by 1768 he was being paid a retainer of £5 a year by the Duke of Atholl to play at family entertainments. At one such – the duke's birthday celebrations in 1783 – he and another fiddler played almost continuously from 1 p.m. until 4 a.m., some fifteen hours. When this photograph was taken a century after Gow's death the cottage still retained its thatched roof. The cottage survives today, although slated, and any fiddle player now would sadly have to compete with the roar of traffic from the A9 in its cutting nearby.

'A lovely scene, and the delight of every traveller who visits it' was how the minister of Little Dunkeld described this view in the *Statistical Account* of the 1790s. Although on the west side of the River Tay, this location – where the River Braan cascades down through a rocky gorge towards the larger river – was within the pleasure grounds of Dunkeld House and could be reached from the house by the ferry at Inver. By the time the minister wrote, the natural beauties of the place had been enhanced by the rustic bridge seen here and the cliff-top summer house to which it gave access. This was known as Ossian's Hall, or The Hermitage, and it provided visitors – of which there were many – with an excellent viewpoint of the falls. But first they were ushered into an ante-room, with a large portrait of the legendary Ossian opposite. This suddenly parted in two, the halves moving sideways to reveal the viewing chamber, of which the walls and ceiling were lined with mirrors, so that onlookers when they entered seemed to find themselves in the midst of waterfalls all around. Impressive, but not everyone appreciated the theatricality. William Wordsworth and his sister Dorothy, visiting in 1803, 'laughed heartily', and Queen Victoria, arriving in the dusk of a damp October afternoon in 1865, noted the 'looking-glasses' and 'painted walls', but found it equally important to record in her journal that 'we took tea almost in the dark'. The portrait was lost in 1869 when the building was partly blown up at the time of riots over tolls on Dunkeld Bridge (see the next page). The mirrors were lost to vandals in 1930 although the building was restored, in simplified form, in 1951 – the second room becoming an open viewing platform – and is now in the care of the National Trust for Scotland.

Alexander Robertson, a native of Dunkeld, was a larger-than-life character – capable, flamboyant, opinionated, and eventually it seems unstable. After working in a bank he set himself up in business as a dealer in coal, wood, lime and potatoes to such good effect that he was able build this grand residence, 'Dundonachie', on the hillside where Strathbraan meets the valley of the Tay. In the 1860s he also played a leading part in campaigning for removal of Dunkeld Bridge tolls. Starting decorously enough as convener of a meeting held to protest against the Duke of Atholl's refusal to receive a deputation from the Free Church, which sought passage for its members without payment on their way to and from worship, he was a short time later to be found furiously attacking the toll gate itself with an axe. Nor was he alone in such activity – there were riots, and prison sentences (though not for Robertson). Bearing in mind the previous page, is it perhaps also relevant that Dundonachie house is not far from the Hermitage? Robertson's campaign was eventually successful and there is more about it on page 29. 'Dundonachie' is also noteworthy for quite a different reason. It was at this location, or one very close by with the same view up the Tay valley to the Grampians beyond, that Millais painted one of his best known pictures of the district, *Over the Hills and Far Away*.

Trochry Post Office, pictured sometime before 1910. The name MacGregor appears over the door and in 1899 the name of the postmaster was recorded as J. R. MacGregor. Letters arrived from Dunkeld at 8.30 a.m. and were dispatched at 3.50 p.m. By 1923 Mrs C. G. M'Farlane was sub-postmistress and there was still a post office in Trochry in the 1960s, at which time it was to be found within a farmhouse.

Trochry Woollen Mill was evidently in the same ownership as the post office, for an 1899 directory records 'John R. M'Gregor' as a woollen manufacturer and dyer, while in the previous photograph the words 'Tweed & Flannel Warehouse' can just be discerned on two of the boards above the one inscribed 'Trochry Post Office' – the building can be seen in the background of the present picture. The mill lade was bringing water from the Braan some distance upstream. The mill had closed by the 1960s, although the mill wheel was still present in the 1970s.

Trochry, viewed from the main road between Dunkeld and Crieff. The scene remains recognisable, but changed methods of farming mean there is no longer a farmyard full of haystacks and the yard itself has become part of the garden for Meikle Trochry farmhouse on the left.

Below: Victorian and Edwardian tourists – having walked through the Duke of Atholl's parkland at Dunkeld, visited the cathedral, crossed the Tay by ferry and ascended to the Hermitage – were encouraged to continue up the Braan for another half hour as far as the Rumbling Bridge. Here, according to Baedeker, they would find a 'romantic waterfall in a narrow gorge'. Millais, however, although resident nearby at Rumbling Bridge cottage for a while, eschewed this viewpoint and positioned himself beyond the bridge, looking upstream at the river tumbling among its rocky islets, to paint *The Sound of Many Waters*. From the bridge itself, even in times of low water, the river can be heard to pass through its gorge below with a satisfactory roar.

Left: Drumour Lodge, seen here beyond the bridge which still carries the Dunkeld – Crieff road over the Braan, was built by the Stewarts of Murthly. In the 1880s it was described as the lodge for one of the finest shootings in the country. In 1899 it was the residence of a Captain Higson and in 1923 of J. F. Mason. In 1978 it was purchased from Murthly Estates to become Corbenic Camphill Community for people with learning difficulties, which continues to flourish there.

Drumour School served a large area – children walked as much as seven miles to reach it. The schoolhouse adjoined the school proper. In 1899 the mistress was Miss Forbes and in 1923 it was a Miss Fyfe. However, the school closed long ago and the building is now a private house.

The house called Eastwood looks out over the Tay to the east of Dunkeld. This is it in 1925, but its particular claim to fame is that some years earlier, in 1893, it was taken for the summer by a wealthy Londoner who was in the habit of taking a house in the district, with his family, for three months each year. He was Rupert Potter and so it was here on 4 September of that year, when the visit was almost over, that his daughter Beatrix sat down to write a letter to a young friend who was ill in bed. For want of anything better to write about, she told him a story – and illustrated it with sketches – about four young rabbits. Of these the antics of the naughtiest, whose name was Peter, will have struck a chord with the millions of children who have read the story, or had it read to them, ever since: for this letter was the original version of *The Tale of Peter Rabbit*.

'Anyone for tennis?' somebody had obviously suggested earlier, and now this happy group is strolling back to Dunkeld after a visit to Birnam and Dunkeld Recreation Ground which, in 1923, offered tennis, cricket, football and bowling. In the middle distance is a Fiat fourteen-seater charabanc of 1921, one of the Scottish Motor Traction's fleet, known as 'Brownies' because of their livery. It is halted at the entrance to the Garden Tea Room and no doubt its passengers would soon be enjoying tea within, for the tea room made a point of catering for excursion parties. The car on the left, with a Paisley registration, is probably a Bullnose Morris. Towering over the scene, on its knoll in the middle distance, is the then-new war memorial.

In 1923 the Garden Tea Room (see inside front cover) advertised its ideal surrounding of 'flower and foliage' with ample indoor and outdoor accommodation for large parties and 'speed service' by experienced assistants – tea in a moment, with own-grown strawberries a speciality. Today the site is occupied by the recent development of houses in traditional style called Bruce Gardens. The peaceful atmosphere the location had once been the scene of riots in 1868, when agitation for removal of the bridge toll was at its height. Three local men (but not Alexander Robertson) were charged with mobbing and rioting, and with breach of the peace. On the first, most serious, charge the jury eventually returned by a majority the good old Scottish verdict of 'not proven', but all three were convicted of breach of the peace and served prison sentences.

By the early 1900s when this photograph was taken, Dunkeld and Birnam Station had long since become a through station on the line from Perth to Inverness. But when it was originally opened in 1856 – the ornate station building on the left dates from this period – it was the terminus of a smaller undertaking, the Perth and Dunkeld Railway. This had been backed by the Earl of Mansfield, of Scone Castle near Perth, and by Sir William Stewart of Murthly Castle; however, the Duke of Atholl would not have the railway on his land. Thus, the station is almost a mile short of Dunkeld itself and it is noteworthy that the platform-end, just behind the photographer, lies within feet of the Inchewan Burn, the boundary between the Murthly and Atholl estates. In its early days the station had both bookstall and refreshment room; today, the whole station building is rented out.

Park View is the central block of the three which line Station Road, Birnam, in the photograph on the back cover. Stewart's shop on the left seemed to have combined the roles of dressmaker, tailor, linen draper and dyer's agent.

The Birnam Hotel was built by Sir William Stewart in, probably, the 1850s: a grand centrepiece for his new village, fronting onto the Perth Road and close to the foot of Station Road. In the 1890s it was being operated by Edward Cesari. Cesari had been manager of the Highland Railway's prestigious Station Hotel at Inverness, and had risen to be in control of all the company's catering; his employers permitted him to run the Birnam Hotel on his own account. Then in 1897, following a dispute with the railway company over shortages of its stocks and crockery, he left under a cloud, but moved to Birnam permanently and apparently satisfactorily. In 1912 the Birnam Hotel suffered a serious fire – see the pictures on the opposite page – but it was rebuilt just in time, as it would seem, to be used as a hospital during the First World War. The rebuilding was on 'up-to-date lines' and in 1923, the year before this photograph was taken, a local guidebook enthused that it was fitted throughout with electric light, had an up-to-date central heating system, and sanitary arrangements 'of the most perfect design'. By then the proprietor was Roger Gillies, and in this picture one of his guests has arrived in a landaulet which may well be a Rolls Royce, while a local tradesman appears to be making his delivery by Fort Model T van. In 1930 there was another fire: damage was mostly confined to the hotel garage, but several vehicles within were destroyed. In the mid 1930s the rate for room and breakfast was around 11s 6d.

By night the Birnam Hotel fire of 12 September 1912 must have been a horrifying spectacle, and by day the full extent of the damage was revealed. During the rebuilding, completed in 1914, the opportunity was taken to make several alterations, and in particular to enlarge some of the windows and allow more light within, as can be seen by comparing the picture below with the one opposite which shows the hotel as rebuilt. As long before as 1882, Blackwood's Magazine had criticised 'the hyper-ecclesiastical narrowness' of the windows to the dining hall.

Col. W. T. J. Steuart Fothringham of Murthly Castle leads a detachment of Scottish Horse through Birnam in 1915. The Scottish Horse were the yeomanry regiment raised locally. Despite being shown mounted here, they would soon find themselves fighting as infantry at Gallipoli. The gates in the background were erected by one of Col. Steuart Fothringham's forebears, and were intended as the entrance to a very long driveway to Murthly Castle.

The Scottish Horse, originally formed in South Africa during the Boer War but disbanded at its end, reappeared in 1903 when Lord Tullibardine, who later became Duke of Atholl, was appointed to raise eight squadrons of Imperial Yeomanry from Perthshire and other parts of rural Scotland. They were named the Scottish Horse. This photograph, which is dated before 1905, must show one of their earliest camps: it is probably at Dunkeld, where they would camp annually, but could also perhaps be Blair Atholl. Despite fighting as infantry during the First World War, the Scottish Horse were again horsed subsequently, and continued cavalry training until as late as February 1940 – after which they were converted into regiments of the Royal Artillery for which there was evidently more demand. But they retained their 'Scottish Horse' identity and fought with valour through the Second World War.

Birnam Highland Games were first held in 1864, although there had been earlier games in Dunkeld. This is the Birnam event of 1872. At this period competitions typically included piping, dancing, vaulting, races, rifle shooting and tilting on horseback. A special train would bring spectators from Perth. At that date photographic techniques seem unlikely to have been adequate for producing photographs of competitors in action, such as later became familiar, and this is probably why the photographer has taken a group photograph of competitors in their best Highland Dress gathered on and around the dais. That they are competitors, and some of them very successful ones, can be ascertained from the quantities of winners' medals that some of them are sporting. Long horsehair sporrans were then popular.

Birnam Oak, in the foreground, was at one time thought to be about 1,000 years old and a relic of the Birnam Wood of Macbeth's day, made famous by Shakespeare. It may in fact not be quite as old as the eleventh century when Macbeth actually reigned, but it is certainly very old, and very big. It was already famous for size and antiquity by the mid nineteenth century and became a regular attraction for tourist visitors. Beyond it is to be seen a very large sycamore, a youngster of some 200 years at the date of the photograph. Both trees survive, the oak with some of its lower branches propped up or removed, but their open setting close to the Tay has been replaced by scrub woodland. In the year 2000 local schoolchildren collected acorns from the oak in order to plant them and perpetuate it.

Murthly Terrace, Birnam, was built by Sir William Stewart in the 1860s but is seen here around the 1920s. It lines the Park Road and has altered little down the years. The drinking fountain, which appears also on page 32, was an addition of about 1914.

At the approach to Birnam from Perth, the villas on the right were built about 1900. Beyond them can be seen the tower of St Mary's Episcopal Church, a truncated view of Murthly Terrace and a projecting gable-end of the Birnam Hotel. The finial atop the hotel's gable-end disappeared in the 1912 fire.

The wooded eminence of Torwood (or Torr) Hill, just to the east of Birnam village, became the setting for a series of sumptuous Victorian villas. In this view, taken presumably from a point high on the slopes of Birnam Hill, can be seen, from left to right, Dunairds (with, beyond it, Eastwood on the far side of the concealed River Tay), Ladyhill, Birchwood House, St Mary's Tower, and Erigmore. The latter two appear in subsequent pictures. All give the impression of having been built with an eye to seasonal lets as much as permanent residence.

St Mary's Tower was built by Lord John Manners, noted Victorian politician who eventually succeeded his brother as Duke of Rutland. Here he entertained the Marquess of Salisbury when Prime Minister, and here he and Lady Manners were photographed by Rupert Potter, skilled amateur photographer in the days when photography was still young, and father of Beatrix. Perhaps the most lasting of the famous names connected with St Mary's Tower is that of John Everett Millais, who took it for the autumn several times in the 1870s and painted many of his best-known Scottish landscapes in the vicinity. He also painted the spiral stair, intending that it should form the background to his painting *The Princes in the Tower*. Then he dispatched his son to visit the Tower of London in search of authenticity, and learned that he had painted a stair that was the wrong way round and too small. So he started all over again. He re-used the original canvas for another painting and the appearance of the St Mary's Tower stair in a Millais painting was lost to posterity, which is a pity, for the later history of the building is less satisfactory. Although it had been converted into flats in 1950, by 1954 it was described in the *Perthshire Advertiser* as acquiring the reputation of being 'the house that nobody wants'. Subsequently it was demolished.

Erigmore was built in the 1860s and, like St Mary's Tower, rented on occasion by Millais. In 1899 it was occupied by Sir Charles B. Logan and in 1923 by a Col. Ferris. Then in 1925 Mrs Ferris evidently decided to sell up – one may hazard a guess that she had been widowed – and on 28 November the *Perthshire Advertiser* carried an advertisement for the sale by auction of what appear to be the entire furniture and furnishings. The list gives a good idea of how these big houses were fitted out, starting with 'a particularly fine 7ft fine walnut bookcase . . . in the Queen Anne style', continuing through the grand piano and the 'whole furnishings of the billiard room' including its full-size table, to a bronze bust of Queen Victoria and a bamboo gong stand, and eventually to the iron bedsteads of the servants' bedrooms, the garden tools and an 'excellent portable henhouse'. The whole list takes up a column and a half. Erigmore was in the *Perthshire Advertiser* again on 21 April 1992 when Erigmore House Holiday Park announced the opening of a £300,000 leisure complex including indoor swimming pool, sauna and jacuzzi. The house continues to be the central component of an immaculate leisure park with lodges, caravans, apartments and holiday accommodation – and so perhaps continues to serve a function akin to that for which it was built, but in a manner appropriate to more egalitarian times.

Rohallion Lodge was built on the southern slopes of Birnam Hill in 1843 for Sir William Stewart. He had inherited Murthly Castle a few years earlier, but before that had spent many years in the American West, at a period when it was still Wild, so perhaps he fancied an informal alternative to the grandeur of centuries-old Murthly. At any rate one of the features of Rohallion was a herd of buffalo imported by Sir William, no doubt as a memento of his time in America. At Rohallion his architect provided him with a shooting lodge in such an eclectic mix of styles that in the 1970s it was able to double as a German castle for a television programme, the makers of which wished to avoid the expense of the real thing. This is one of many entertaining tales of life there at that period told by Douglas Sutherland in his book *Rohallion*.

Snaigow House, east of Dunkeld and north of Caputh, was built in the 1820s. By 1899 it was the residence of William H. Cox, who was still there in 1923. Cox was a Dundee jute magnate and chairman of the Highland Railway Company from 1916 until its dissolution in 1923. One of its locomotives was named *Snaigow* after the chairman's residence and, coincidentally, the present author included an illustration of this in an earlier book, *Iron Road: The Railway in Scotland*. In 1960, according to Haynes *Illustrated Architectural Guide*, Snaigow House was found to be infested with dry rot: it was demolished and a replacement (which included the staircase of the old house) was built on the same site.

Butterstone House was built in the 1860s for Lord Armitstead and altered in the 1890s. Here he entertained W. E. Gladstone. It later passed into the hands of the Crabbie family, whose fortune was based on ginger wine, subsequently to the Lyle family (sugar), and then to the Linklater family whose property it remains. By the date of this photograph, 1952, Butterstone House School, a girls' preparatory school, had recently been established there. This school eventually moved away about 1990, and in its place Veronica Linklater established The New School to provide children with special needs, aged twelve and upwards, with the support they require. The New School has recently celebrated twenty successful years; the house externally is little altered.

In 1901, the approximate date of this picture, Butterstone Post Office, seen here, was located in Craigton Cottage at the east end of the village. At that period Dunkeld Post Office despatched the letters to Butterstone at 7.30 a.m. while outward letters from Butterstone arrived at Dunkeld at 1.30 p.m.

This is the view looking west through Butterstone village in the years before 1929. On the left are the school and school house, where Jane Reid was the mistress in 1899 and Mrs Thomson in 1923. The row of houses on the right includes the smithy, seen better in the next picture.

Butterstone in 1904, with the smithy on the right. At that date the blacksmith was Peter Carr, so we are probably looking at his wife and family. The agricultural implements, which include ploughs and harrows, may well have been part of his stock-in-trade – it seems unlikely that all were present for repairs.